Dear Parent:
Your child's love of reading starts here!

Every child learns to read in a different way and at his or her own speed. Some go back and forth between reading levels and read favorite books again and again. Others read through each level in order. You can help your young reader improve and become more confident by encouraging his or her own interests and abilities. From books your child reads with you to the first books he or she reads alone, there are I Can Read Books for every stage of reading:

SHARED READING
Basic language, word repetition, and whimsical illustrations, ideal for sharing with your emergent reader

BEGINNING READING
Short sentences, familiar words, and simple concepts for children eager to read on their own

READING WITH HELP
Engaging stories, longer sentences, and language play for developing readers

READING ALONE
Complex plots, challenging vocabulary, and high-interest topics for the independent reader

I Can Read Books have introduced children to the joy of reading since 1957. Featuring award-winning authors and illustrators and a fabulous cast of beloved characters, I Can Read Books set the standard for beginning readers.

A lifetime of discovery begins with the magical words **"I Can Read!"**

Visit www.icanread.com for information
on enriching your child's reading experience.

Visit www.zonderkidz.com/icanread for more faith-based
I Can Read! titles from Zonderkidz.

"Who knows? It's possible that you became queen
for a time just like this."

—Esther 4:14

ZONDERKIDZ

The Beginner's Bible Queen Esther Saves Her People
Copyright © 2018 by Zondervan
Illustrations © 2018 by Zondervan

An **I Can Read Book**

Requests for information should be addressed to:
Zonderkidz, 3900 Sparks Drive SE, Grand Rapids, Michigan 49546

ISBN 978-0-310-76478-6

Illustrator: Denis Alonso

Printed in the United States of America

23 24 25 CWM 10 9 8 7 6 5 4 3

ZONDERkidz™

SHARED READING

My First

I Can Read!

The Beginner's Bible®

Queen Esther Saves Her People

ZONDERkidz™

Once there was a king
who needed a new queen.

"Let us find you
a new queen," said
the king's men.

Esther and Mordecai were
cousins. They lived in
the king's land.

They loved God.

Mordecai said,
"You could be the new queen."

So Esther got ready.

And she went to see the king.

The king liked Esther.

He said, "Will you be my queen?

Esther said, "Yes."

The king had a helper.

His name was Haman.

He was a mean man.

Esther and her cousin were Jewish.
Haman hated Jewish people.
He did not love God.

Haman had a plan.
He went to the king.

The king did not know
Queen Esther was Jewish.
The king was tricked!

God's people were in danger!
Mordecai heard about the plan.

Mordecai went to tell Esther.

"Esther! Save God's people.
Maybe that is why
God made you the queen!"

Esther needed a plan.

It would not be easy.

But Esther was brave.

She would help God's people.

Esther made a nice dinner.

She invited the king and Haman.

The king and Haman were happy.
The king asked, "What can I do
for you, Esther?"

"Haman tricked you!
You signed a law," Esther
said.

"It says to get rid of all Jews.
I am Jewish!"

The king was mad!
He did not like to be tricked.

The king said, "Get Haman!
Arrest him now!"

The king made Mordecai his new helper.

The king was happy with Mordecai.
The king was happy with Esther.

The Jewish people were saved!

Esther was a hero.

God used Esther
to save his people.